The Mystery
of the
Hidden Letter

By Nancy Antle
Illustrated by Laurie Harden

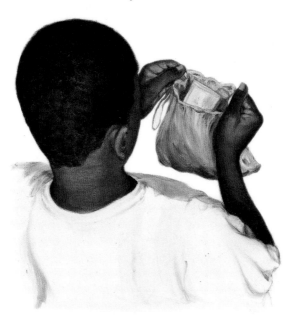

CELEBRATION PRESS
Pearson Learning Group

Contents

~ Chapter 1 ~
The Secret Panel

Curtis swept a pile of dirt and grit into the dustpan his sister, Faith, was holding.

"I hope this is clean enough for Grandma," Curtis said.

"She is kind of picky," Faith laughed.

"I don't know why she cares," Curtis said. "because no one's going to see how clean the living room is but us."

Curtis and Faith were helping their grandparents move into their new home outside Tonapah, a small town in the Nevada desert. The house had once belonged to Grandpa's great-great-great-uncle, William Clarke, who was one of the first African Americans to settle in Nevada.

"It's an odd old house," Faith commented.

Curtis couldn't argue with that because the house had staircases that went nowhere and doors that opened onto solid walls. There was even a secret hiding place under the stairs.

Curtis even liked looking at the giant map that Great-Uncle William had painted on one wall of the living room. Most of Nevada's cities were on the map—even Las Vegas, where Curtis and Faith lived with their mom and dad.

Even though the house was interesting, Curtis had explored every inch of it in two days. The biggest problem with the house was that it was a long way from town and there was nothing to do.

Curtis looked out the window and sighed. There was nothing but sagebrush and rocks as far as he could see. What was he going to do here for three whole weeks?

"This must be the dullest place on Earth," Curtis grumbled.

"Nonsense," Grandma said coming into the living room with Grandpa. "There are plenty of rooms to clean and porches to paint." She winked, and Faith grinned.

Curtis hadn't meant for his grandparents to overhear what he had said. "I like your house," he said quickly, embarrassed. "It's just so far from anything fun to do."

"Don't worry," Grandpa said. "We're going to take you to do something fun right now."

"Just as soon as you get that last spider web over there," Grandma directed Curtis.

"I told you she was picky," Faith whispered.

Grandpa laughed, then whispered back, "and you were right."

Curtis laughed, too. He walked to the corner of the room where Grandma had pointed. He was too short to reach the ceiling—even holding the broom over his head. He jumped as high as he could and swatted the ceiling with the broom—hard.

Before Curtis really knew what was happening, there was a creaking sound. Then a little trapdoor opened in the tin ceiling, and something fell out right on Curtis's head.

"Are you okay?" Grandma and Faith asked at the same time. They both rushed over to Curtis to see if he was badly hurt.

Curtis rubbed his head and nodded.

"What happened?" Grandpa asked.

"I guess I opened some kind of secret panel in the ceiling," Curtis answered. Then he bent down, picked up the leather pouch that was lying on the floor, and said, "This was in it."

Curtis reached into the pouch, where he found a metal spike the size of a pencil. There was also a piece of paper inside. Curtis unfolded it and stared. A lot of fancy writing filled the paper, and it was signed, *William Clarke*. Suddenly, Grandma and Grandpa's house had become a whole lot more interesting!

Chapter 2

The Letter

"Read what it says," Faith said.

"We're all ears," Grandpa added as Grandma smiled encouragingly.

Curtis cleared his throat and began reading, "October 11, 1910. I hope one of my kin finds this letter. I never did spend my treasure, so it's still where I left it, I hope. Here are the clues: The Comstock, New York, and a Chinese gate."

"I don't get it," Faith said.

"There's more," Curtis said, as he read on. "Remember to look at the map so you always know where you are, and use the spike to point the way. Good luck, William Clarke."

"Looks like we have a real mystery on our hands," Grandpa said.

"Do you think Great-Uncle William really hid a treasure?" Faith asked.

"It's probably just another one of his jokes," Curtis said, "like the stairs and doors that don't lead anywhere."

"Maybe," Grandma said.

"Or, maybe not," Grandpa disagreed.

"Why didn't he spend the treasure?" Curtis asked. "Why leave it for someone to find later?"

Grandpa sat down on a chair, followed by Grandma. Curtis and Faith sat down on the sofa. Curtis knew to get comfortable because Grandpa was about to tell a story.

"Great-Uncle William was born into slavery. Then, right before the American Civil War started, he was set free," Grandpa said.

"Great-Uncle William was a slave?" Curtis asked.

"He must have been happy to be set free," Faith added.

Grandma nodded. "Great-Uncle William came west to seek his fortune, but he was afraid of being made a slave again. That's why this house has fake stairways and a secret room."

"So, Great-Uncle William did all that stuff to his house to confuse anyone who was after him?" Curtis asked.

Grandma gently poked Curtis in the chest, and said, "Exactly."

"Did he come to Nevada to look for gold?" Faith asked.

"He did, but he didn't find any, so he opened a barbershop instead," Grandpa explained.

"How could Great-Uncle William afford a house like this?" Curtis asked. "This looks like it was a rich person's house."

"It was," Grandpa said. "In the early days of Nevada, barbers were often the leaders of the African American community. They knew everyone and everything that was going on."

"People came to them sometimes for loans," Grandma said.

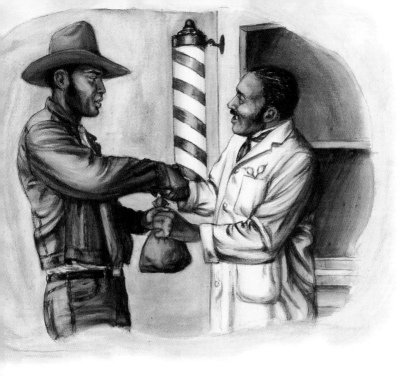

"Seems like that would make you poor," Faith said, "not rich."

"That's for sure," Curtis added.

"Great-Uncle William loaned a friend some money to stake a claim to a gold mine," Grandpa explained. "When his friend struck it rich, he gave Great-Uncle William half."

"Did he find a lot of gold?" Curtis asked.

"He surely did," Grandpa said.

"Didn't Great-Uncle William spend it?" Faith asked.

"All the family stories I have heard say that he lived quite well," Grandma said.

"Maybe he hid some of the gold in case he needed to run away someday," Curtis suggested.

Grandpa nodded, then added, "Maybe so."

Curtis held up Great-Uncle William's letter. "If there really is a treasure to find," he said, "we have to figure out what all the clues mean as soon as possible."

Grandpa took the letter from Curtis and read it again. "You know what the Comstock is, don't you?" Grandpa asked.

"It's one of the first silver mines in Nevada," Curtis said. "I learned about it in school."

"That's right," Grandpa said. " and it was probably the biggest silver mine ever anywhere."

"Can we go there?" Faith asked as she jumped up from the sofa.

"The old Comstock mine is near Virginia City, which is hundreds of miles from here," Grandma said, "but we could take you to another old silver mine if you want." She winked at Grandpa.

"Right now?" Curtis asked.

"The car is waiting," Grandpa said.

"Yippee!" Curtis and Faith both yelled together, as they raced outside.

As they left, Curtis noticed a black car down the road from his grandparents' house. *Must be lost tourists*, he thought to himself. After a short while, Curtis had forgotten about it. As he peered out the window of his grandparents' car, he wondered if Nevada looked the same today as it did when Great-Uncle William was alive.

The leather pouch they'd found sat on Curtis's lap. He reached inside and took out the folded paper. He read Great-Uncle William's words again. "Here are the clues: The Comstock, New York, and a Chinese gate. Remember to look at the map so you always know where you are, and use the spike to point the way."

What could it all mean? Curtis thought as he rubbed his finger over the smooth metal spike. *How could it point the way?* Nothing made any sense.

"Curtis, look!" Faith exclaimed. "There's a town ahead."

Curtis looked back out the window. He saw a dirt street with old wooden buildings on either side that all seemed about to fall over.

"That's not a real town," Curtis said.

"It's a ghost town," Grandpa said.

"What's a ghost town?" Faith asked.

"It's just a town where no one lives anymore," Grandma said.

"Some people claim to see ghosts in ghost towns, but I never have," Grandpa said laughing. Faith and Curtis chuckled, too.

"Why did the people leave this town?" Curtis asked.

"The town was built when there were a lot of gold and silver mines nearby," Grandma explained. "Then when the gold and silver ran out, the people left, too, because they could no longer make a living."

"Is this where Great-Uncle William had his barbershop?" Faith asked.

"Yup," Grandpa replied.

"Can we stop and look at it?" Curtis asked. "Maybe we'll find more clues about where the treasure is."

"There's not much to see," Grandpa said, "but we can stop if you want."

When Grandpa stopped the car, Curtis and Faith scrambled out of the back seat. They followed Grandpa and Grandma to the building that said *Barbershop* over the door.

"This is it," Grandpa said.

They all walked up the steps and through the open door. Inside they saw a cracked, dusty mirror on one wall, and a broken chair with only three legs in one corner. In another corner was a rusty bucket.

"Maybe we'll see Great-Uncle William's ghost," Faith giggled.

"I don't think so," Grandma said. "There is no such thing as a ghost."

"I wish Great-Uncle William himself was here," Curtis sighed, "so I could ask him what his letter means."

"That's not possible either," Faith said to her brother in a teasing tone.

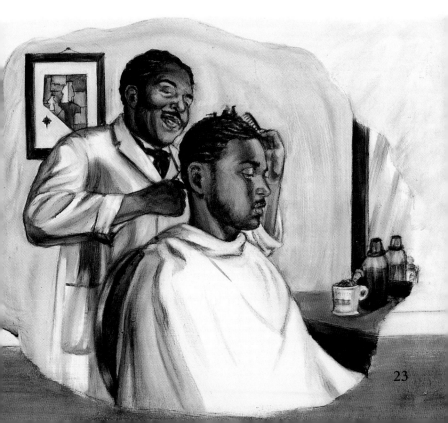

"Isn't that another map?" Curtis asked, pointing to a crooked picture frame hanging on the far wall. The map was old, faded, and dusty.

"It sure is," Grandpa said, "and it looks kind of like the one in the living room at home."

A sudden gust of wind whistled through the broken windows, and it blew the map onto the floor with a loud bang, making everyone jump at the sound. Curtis thought with a shiver that maybe it was Great-Uncle William.

"It's just the wind," Grandma said as Curtis walked over to the map, picked it up, and noticed the name of a town—Manhattan.

"Look," he said pointing to Manhattan. "Isn't that the name of a place in New York?"

"Right," Grandpa agreed. "Manhattan, Nevada, is on our map at home, too."

"Maybe all the clues are a code for towns in Nevada," Curtis said. "Maybe we have to visit three towns in Nevada."

"Good thinking," Grandma said, "but I don't know any town with a Chinese gate."

"I don't either," Grandpa said, "but we could ask Sam about it when we see him."

"Who's Sam?" Curtis asked.

"He's a good friend, who owns the land next to ours," Grandma said. "The silver mine we told you about is on his land."

"Also, Sam used to teach at the university," Grandpa continued, "and he's an expert on Nevada and its history. If anyone can help us understand the clues, it will be Sam."

Chapter 4
Sam and the Silver Mine

As they headed back to the car, Curtis noticed the same black car he had seen before.

"Grandpa, I saw that same car near your house earlier today," said Curtis.

"Probably some tourists," said Grandpa.

Curtis wanted to think Grandpa was right, but he wasn't convinced. He looked back again—the car was gone!

For a while, the mysterious black car was forgotten as they rode over a very bumpy dirt road. Finally, Grandma stopped the car in front of an old shack next to a hill. A bearded man walked out of a tunnel dug into the side of the hill and waved. Everyone scrambled out of the car to greet Sam.

Faith spoke first. "Hi, I'm Faith. Great-Uncle William's ceiling fell on my brother's head, and we visited a ghost town and found a map. Now we have a big mystery to solve."

"Whew," Sam said as he grinned. "You are having a real adventure, aren't you?"

Grandma told Sam about the secret panel, then Curtis showed him the letter they had found. Sam read it and scratched his forehead.

"That's a real mystery, all right."

"We think Great-Uncle William means three different towns in Nevada," Curtis told him. "The Comstock means Virginia City and New York means Manhattan."

"I think you're right," Sam said. "but what about this Chinese gate?"

"We were hoping you would know a town that has one," Faith said.

Sam grinned. "Let me think on it while I show you the silver mine."

At the entrance to the mine, Sam handed them each a flashlight and a miner's hard hat.

"Is this as big as the Comstock?" Curtis asked.

"This is a just a baby mine compared to the Comstock," Sam answered. "The tunnel the miners dug there was longer than the Empire State Building is tall."

"That's amazing!" exclaimed Curtis.

"I'll tell you something else that is amazing," Sam added, "The first Comstock miners were looking for gold, so they threw away tons of sticky blue mud that kept getting in their way."

"Why was it blue?" Faith asked.

"Guess," Sam said.

"Silver?" Curtis asked.

"That's right," Sam said. "It just took them awhile to figure it out."

The tunnel became darker and darker the farther into it they went. Curtis remembered seeing an old movie about mining in which the miners were trapped when the tunnel caved in.

"Is this tunnel safe?" Curtis asked nervously.

Grandpa shined his flashlight up to the ceiling. "See all those wooden beams up there?" he pointed out. "Those timbers brace the tunnel and keep it from falling on top of us."

"The historical society has done some work on this mine," Sam said. "We hope to open it for tours in a few months. However, most all of the old, abandoned mines around here aren't safe for anyone to go into."

Finally, Sam stopped. There was a big metal spike and a sledgehammer leaning against the mine wall. "I'm going to show you how the miners drilled holes," he said .

Sam picked up the spike, pointed it into the rock wall, and hit it. *Whack!* The sound echoed through the tunnel.

"Want to try?" Sam asked Curtis.

As Curtis took the spike and hammer from Sam, he found it was hard to lift them. He hit the spike. *Ping!* Everyone laughed, even Curtis.

"After the miners drilled the holes, they put in sticks of dynamite," Sam said. "Then they lit the dynamite and ran."

"That must've been scary," Faith said.

"That's for sure, but I bet they had a blast," Curtis joked, and everyone laughed again.

Grandpa asked, "After the dynamite went off, what did they do?"

"They hauled all the rubble out in carts," Sam answered. "Then wagons took the rock to mills where the silver was extracted."

"Did everyone get rich?" Faith asked.

"The mine owners got rich," Sam said. "but the miners barely made enough to live on."

Curtis thought about what a difficult job mining must have been. He was glad that his great-uncle had been a barber, not a miner.

Back outside, Sam tossed the spike and hammer onto the ground near the entrance. The bright sunshine made Curtis squint. Then he looked at the spike and got an idea.

Curtis showed Sam the spike from the leather pouch. Sam put it next to the one they had used inside the mine.

"Looks like you have your own little miner's spike," he said, "but this one's silver."

Curtis looked at the dull, gray spike in his hand. "Really?" he asked, thrilled.

Sam nodded. "Use a little silver polish on it," he said, "and you'll get a nice surprise."

Curtis shook his head as he walked to the car. *If the spike was silver, did that mean Great-Uncle William had silver hidden somewhere?* he thought. *Was he ever going to figure out what town in Nevada had a Chinese gate?* Curtis wished he knew.

Curtis's grandparents invited Sam to drive home with them and stay for supper. They all piled into the car and headed for home. Curtis was just drifting off to sleep when he glanced out the window and saw in the distance the same black car he had seen twice earlier in the day. He was sure the car was following them.

~ Chapter 5 ~
The Treasure

Suddenly, Sam let out a *whoop!* "I know what town Great-Uncle William meant for 'Chinese gate!'" he said.

"What? What?" Curtis asked. Once again, the strange black car was forgotten. Instead, Curtis wanted to hear what Sam had to say about the Chinese gate.

"There's a town up north called Beowawe," Sam said. "Beowawe is a Native American word. It means 'gate.'"

"That's not Chinese," Faith said.

"No," Sam said, "but most likely the first people to settle in Beowawe were from China. They went there to help build the western railroad."

"Perfect!" Curtis said.

When they got home, Curtis rushed to the living room to look at the big map of Nevada. Everyone followed close behind.

"Can you show me where Beowawe is?" Curtis asked Sam.

Sam pointed to a place on the map. Then Curtis found Virginia City and Manhattan on the map, too.

"Great-Uncle William's letter said to look at the map," Curtis said. "I did that, so now what?"

Sam scratched his chin and shrugged. "Remind me what else the letter says."

36

"Let the spike point the way," Curtis repeated. Then he used the small spike to point first to Virginia City, then Manhattan, and finally Beowawe.

"What did you think that would do?" Faith asked when nothing happened.

"I guess I was hoping that there'd be another secret panel with another letter," Curtis said, disappointed.

"Me, too," Grandpa said.

"It *is* a drilling spike," Sam said.

"Should I drill into the wall?" Curtis asked.

"I'll get you a hammer," Grandma said.

Curtis couldn't believe his picky grandma would let him pound a spike into her wall.

"We'll never figure out Great-Uncle William's clues unless we try something," replied Grandma. She went into the kitchen and came back with a hammer.

Curtis put the spike on the dot that was Virginia City and hammered into it. There was a loud click like someone unlocking a door. Curtis turned to look at the others who all stared at him with wide eyes.

"Keep going," Faith said.

Then Curtis hammered the spike into Manhattan, and everyone heard another loud click. Finally, he hammered into Beowawe, and there was one more click followed by a creaking sound. A door in the wall opened!

"That is *some* secret panel," Sam said.

Curtis peeked around the door and saw stairs leading down. Before he could say a word, Grandpa handed him a flashlight, and they all walked slowly down the dark steps.

"I hope we find bags of gold nuggets," Faith whispered. "We'll be rich."

"Jewels would be nice," Grandma added.

When the steps ended, they found themselves in a basement with a dirt floor.

"Just looks like a dirty, empty basement to me," Grandpa said.

"Look over there," Sam said, pointing to a tunnel that led away from the house. Everyone followed Sam down the tunnel until they came to the end.

"Nothing here," Curtis said. "Someone must have been here before us—a long time ago."

"It feels like I'm stepping on something squishy," Faith said.

They shined their flashlight beams down to the dark and muddy floor of the tunnel. Curtis looked at the mud and then back at Sam, who was grinning.

"Please tell me that's blue mud," Curtis said, "like you said they found in the Comstock mines."

"Yes," Sam grinned. "I believe it is."

"We found Great-Uncle William's treasure!" Faith yelled.

"We found Great-Uncle William's silver mine!" Curtis corrected. Everyone was so excited that they danced in the blue mud.

Then Curtis suddenly stopped and asked. "If Great-Uncle William knew about the silver, why didn't he ever do anything about it?"

"My guess goes back to what I said earlier," Grandma said. "I think he became so afraid of losing what he had that he didn't want to tell anyone about the silver."

When the group returned to the living room, Curtis was the first to notice a black car pull up in the driveway. It was the same black car he'd seen before.

"Oh, no," he said. "That's the car that has been following us."

"Maybe they're going to try to steal our treasure," gasped Faith as they watched two men get out of the car and slowly walk to the front door.

Chapter 6

A Place for Uncle William

There was a knock at the door. Grandpa told everyone to stay in the living room while he answered it.

"Grandpa, you might need help," Curtis pleaded. "What if those men are here to cause trouble?"

"Don't worry. I'll handle it," Grandpa replied as he left the room.

Curtis heard one of the men ask, "Mr. Clarke?" when Grandpa answered the door. Then he said something Curtis couldn't hear.

Then Curtis heard Grandpa say stiffly, "Let's talk about this on the porch."

Curtis and Faith peered through the front curtains trying to see and hear what was going on as the men talked to Grandpa. None of the words were clear, but Curtis did see one of the men unroll a large map and start pointing to something.

A few minutes later, Curtis suddenly heard
Grandpa say, "I don't think I like that idea."

Curtis was about to yell for Grandma to
telephone the police when Grandpa came
back into the living room. Curtis glanced out
the window and saw the men leaving; one of
them carrying the rolled-up map.

"What happened?" everyone said at once.
Grandpa's stern expression changed to a
smile when he saw their anxious faces.

"Those men are geologists," Grandpa explained. "At first, they just wanted to tell me that they planned to make an offer to buy Great-Uncle William's land for a client. I said there would be no discussion of that until I knew all the details. They finally said they have been studying old mining records for a mining company, and they discovered that a vein of silver from an old abandoned mine near here stretches over onto this land."

"What did you say?" Faith asked.

"Well, they seemed surprised when I said I knew about the silver. I didn't say that I had just found out." Everyone laughed.

"The company will pay a lot of money for the land," Grandpa continued. "I said we need to think about what we want to do. Then we'll let them know."

Several nights later, Curtis perched on the front steps of his grandparents' house. It was hard to believe he had ever thought this place was dull, and now, he was sorry the adventure was over.

"What's going to happen to Great-Uncle William's house?" Curtis asked. He was worried, because modern mining involved huge pits and gigantic trucks.

"The mining company is going to need a lot of room," Grandpa said," and the house is sitting almost on top of the silver lode."

"I know," Curtis said, "but it isn't some stranger's house. It's important to us."

Grandma put her arm around Curtis and said, "It's a great old house, isn't it?" Curtis nodded.

"The mining company will give us a share of the profits, and they're paying us now for the right to dig on our land," Grandpa said.

"I'm glad you'll have plenty of money," Curtis said gloomily.

"That's right," Grandma said. "We'll have plenty of money to move the house miles away, and Sam knows a man who can do it."

"Is it really possible to move a whole house?" Curtis asked.

"I'd say Great-Uncle William has shown us that anything is possible," Grandma reassured him.

"That's for sure," Curtis agreed with a big smile.

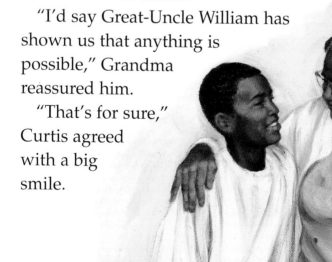